Sonia Sotomayor

U.S. SUPREME COURT JUSTICE

By Alex Van Tol

Crabtree Publishing Company
www.crabtreebooks.com

Crabtree Publishing Company
www.crabtreebooks.com

Author: Alex Van Tol
Publishing plan research and development:
  Sean Charlebois, Reagan Miller
  Crabtree Publishing Company
Editors: Mark Sachner, Lynn Peppas
Indexer: Wendy Scavuzzo
Editorial director: Kathy Middleton
Photo researcher: Ruth Owen
Designer: Alix Wood
Production coordinator: Margaret Amy Salter
Production: Kim Richardson
Prepress technician: Margaret Amy Salter

Written, developed, and produced by
Water Buffalo Books

Cover: Sonia Sotomayor is congratulated by President Barack Obama after being sworn in as the 111th Justice of the U.S. Supreme Court. Not only is she the first person of Hispanic descent to grace the bench, she also brings more federal justice experience with her to the U.S. Supreme Court than any justice has in the past 100 years.

Publisher's note:
All quotations in this book come from original sources and contain the spelling and grammatical inconsistencies of the original text. The use of such constructions is for the sake of preserving the historical and literary accuracy of the sources.

Photographs and reproductions:
Flickr (Creative Commons): page 101
Getty Images: Paul J. Richards: page 5; Spencer Platt: page 15;
  Paul J. Richards: page 19; Al Fenn: page 22; Hulton Archive:
  page 23; Spencer Platt: page 25; Paul J. Richards: page 31;
  Paul J. Richards: page 43; Fred W. McDarrah: page 45;
  Spencer Platt: page 47; Paul J. Richards: page 51; Chris
  Wilkins: page 59; Paul J. Richards: page 61; Paul J.
  Richards: page 73; Paul J. Richards: page 89; Pete Souza:
  page 91; Paul J. Richards: page 93; Spencer Platt: page 98
Shutterstock: page 4 (background); page 9; page 12; page 26;
  page 41; page 48; page 53; page 63; page 67; page 81;
  page 86
White House Photography: Pete Souza: front cover
  (background); Chuck Kennedy: page 1; Lawrence Jackson:
  page 7; Pete Souza: page 17; page 24; Pete Souza: page 29;
  Chuck Kennedy: page 75; Johnny Simon: page 77; Pete Souza:
  page 80; page 99
Wikipedia (public domain): front cover (main); page 4 (inset);
  page 10; page 21; page 27; page 33; page 34; page 37;
  page 39; page 55; page 82; page 85; page 95

Library and Archives Canada Cataloguing in Publication

Van Tol, Alex
    Sonia Sotomayor : U.S. Supreme Court justice / Alex Van Tol.

(Crabtree groundbreaker biographies)
Includes index.
Issued also in an electronic format.
ISBN 978-0-7787-2537-4 (bound).--ISBN 978-0-7787-2546-6 (pbk.)

    1. Sotomayor, Sonia, 1954- --Juvenile literature. 2. United States. Supreme Court--Biography--Juvenile literature.
3. Hispanic American judges--Biography--Juvenile literature.
4. Judges--United States--Biography--Juvenile literature. I. Title.
II. Series: Crabtree groundbreaker biographies

KF8745.S67V35 2011   j347.73'2634   C2010-903026-5

Library of Congress Cataloging-in-Publication Data

Van Tol, Alex.
Sonia Sotomayor : U.S. Supreme Court justice / Alex Van Tol.
    p. cm. -- (Crabtree groundbreaker biographies)
  Includes index.
  ISBN 978-0-7787-2537-4 (reinforced library binding : alk. paper) -- ISBN 978-0-7787-2546-6 (pbk. : alk. paper) --
  ISBN 978-1-4271-9469-5 (electronic : pdf)
 1. Sotomayor, Sonia, 1954---Juvenile literature. 2. Hispanic American judges--Biography--Juvenile literature. 3. Judges--United States--Biography--Juvenile literature. I. Title. II. Series.

KF8745.S67V36 2010
347.73'2634--dc22
[B]
                                                2010018045

Crabtree Publishing Company

Printed in the U.S.A./052014/CJ20140421

www.crabtreebooks.com   1-800-387-7650

Copyright © **2011 CRABTREE PUBLISHING COMPANY.** All rights reserved. No part of this publication may be reproduced, stored in a retrieval system or be transmitted in any form or by any means, electronic, mechanical, photocopying, recording, or otherwise, without the prior written permission of Crabtree Publishing Company. In Canada: We acknowledge the financial support of the Government of Canada through the Canada Book Fund for our publishing activities.

Published in Canada
Crabtree Publishing
616 Welland Ave.
St. Catharines, Ontario
L2M 5V6

Published in the United States
Crabtree Publishing
PMB 59051
350 Fifth Avenue, 59th Floor
New York, New York 10118

Published in the United Kingdom
Crabtree Publishing
Maritime House
Basin Road North, Hove
BN41 1WR

Published in Australia
Crabtree Publishing
3 Charles Street
Coburg North
VIC 3058

Contents

Chapter 1 Nomination to the U.S. Supreme Court!..........4

Chapter 2 Reading *Nancy Drew* in the Projects..........19

Chapter 3 The College Years..........31

Chapter 4 Law and Order on the Streets of New York..........43

Chapter 5 On the Bench at Last..........51

Chapter 6 Life as a Judge in the Court of Appeals..........61

Chapter 7 Nomination to the Supreme Court: The Opportunity of a Lifetime..........73

Chapter 8 The Person Behind the Robe..........93

Chronology..........104

Glossary..........106

Further Information..........108

Index..........110

About the Author..........112

Chapter 1
Nomination to the U.S. Supreme Court!

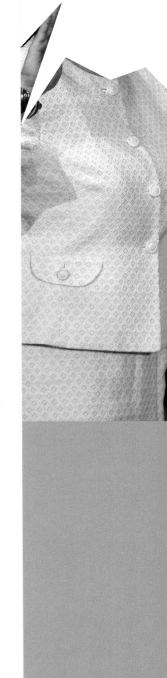

On May 25, 2009, Sonia Sotomayor had a conversation she'd never forget. It was a mild spring evening in New York City. The 54-year-old judge was in her office. She had arrived there at 8 a.m. She had been waiting all day for the call to come through. When the phone on her desk finally rang at 8:10 p.m., the president of the United States was on the other end of the line. "Judge," said President Barack Obama, "I would like to announce you as my selection to be the next Associate Justice of the Supreme Court."

Opposite: A statue based on the concept of justice as (a) blindfolded, (b) holding a set of scales in one hand, and (c) carrying a double-edged sword in the other. This image is meant to portray justice as blind to factors, such as wealth or poverty, that might unfairly influence a decision; prepared to balance arguments on both sides of a case; and ready to wield power on whichever side of the case is deemed right.

The Truth Behind the Rumors

The Supreme Court is the highest court in the country.

Needless to say, it was an exciting moment for Sonia Sotomayor. For weeks up until that day, rumors had been swirling. News had leaked about Justice David Souter's plans to retire from the Supreme Court—and people had been whispering that Sonia Sotomayor was being considered as one of several possible successors for Justice Souter. Sonia was excited by the possibility, but she refused to believe the rumors until she heard the official word.

When the president called, Sonia was nervous. "I had my cellphone in my right hand, and I had my left hand over my chest, trying to calm my beating heart, literally," she said. Being told by the president that he wanted her on the Supreme Court was a heady moment—one she had spent her whole career preparing for. She thanked the president, calling the nomination the most humbling honor of her life.

And then Sonia Sotomayor—in line to become the third woman and the first person of Hispanic descent to serve on the Supreme Court—started to cry.

Opposite: President Barack Obama talks by phone with U.S. Supreme Court Justice nominee Judge Sonia Sotomayor from the Oval Office on Sunday, July 12, 2009—the day before the Senate hearings begin.

Washington Bound

Sonia grabbed the suitcase she had hastily packed earlier that day on the advice of White House staff. She called a friend and asked if he could give her a lift to Washington, D.C. Together, they hit the road. Across the country, Sonia's family and friends had boarded planes and were heading to the capital to join her for the occasion.

Sonia and her friend drove through the night, getting lost and battling torrential rain as they headed to the nation's capital, where the announcement would be made. She was going to be formally nominated to the Supreme Court!

Sonia arrived in Washington at 2:30 in the morning on the day of her nomination. True to her hard-working nature, she practiced her speech for an hour before going to bed. Then she turned out the lights. It was time to try to get some sleep. The next day, Sonia was going to be making history!

It was time to try to get some sleep. The next day, Sonia was going to be making history!

The Justice System

In the United States, the powers that run the nation are separated into three branches: the Executive (the president), the Legislative (the U.S. Congress) and the Judicial (the courts). The Legislative branch makes laws. The Judicial branch interprets, or applies them, to U.S. citizens. The Supreme Court is the primary component of the Judicial branch of government.

Located in the nation's capital of Washington, D.C., the modern-day Supreme Court is housed in a long white building. A vast flight of stairs, many imposing columns, and a set of tall wooden doors greet visitors at the entrance. This is where many of the country's important cases are decided—and it's the last stop for any legal action in the United States of America. Once a case is heard and adjudicated by the Supreme Court, the decision is final—and irrevocable.

The Supreme Court is primarily known as an appellate court. Most cases arrive there after having been tried at other courts such as those at the state or district level. While the Supreme Court does in fact have original jurisdiction over a small number of cases, meaning they'll be heard for the first time at the Supreme Court, most of the cases it hears are appeals. An appeal happens when one or both involved

Just Pay for the Justices

Associate Justices make just over $200,000 a year. The salary of the Chief Justice is even higher—about $250,000. That sounds like a lot—and it is—but consider the job: a huge number of cases—difficult cases that have kept other judges across the country awake at night as they try to arrive at a fair decision. The decisions made by the Supreme Court cannot be appealed or reversed, so they matter more than those at other court levels. It's not an easy job!

One of the roles of the Chief Justice of the Supreme Court is to swear in the president of the United States. Here, in order to avoid any constitutional problems, Chief Justice John G. Roberts Jr. gives the oath of office a second time to Barack Obama in the Map Room of the White House on Wednesday, January 21, 2009.

parties decide they don't like a ruling that's been handed down to them by a lower court and so determine to take it to a higher level.

The Supreme Court is composed of one Chief Justice and eight Associate Justices, for a total of nine judges on the bench. It's important to have an odd number of judges. That way, there can't be any "tie votes" on important decisions. The only person who has the power to nominate judges to the bench is the president of the United States.

The Supreme Court was established in 1790. In the early years, from 1791 to 1801, the court didn't even have its own building. The judges just met at Philadelphia city hall, because at that time, the U.S. capital was Philadelphia. When Washington, D.C., became the capital in 1800, the court moved there, but it still didn't have its own quarters. So the court just shifted around among different spaces within the U.S. Capitol building.

It wasn't until 1935 that the Supreme Court got its very own spot, setting down roots in the striking building it currently inhabits.

Achieving the American Dream

Later that same day, President Obama officially nominated Sonia to the Supreme Court. He explained that he was choosing her for her brilliant legal career, for her "wisdom accumulated from an inspiring life's journey," and for her common touch. "She's faced down barriers, overcome the odds, lived out the American Dream that brought her parents here so long ago," he said to the listening crowd. "And even as she has accomplished so

much in her life, she has never forgotten where she began, never lost touch with the community that supported her." The president went on to say that Sonia's nomination to the Supreme Court was important for another reason. It would be another step for America toward equality. It would bring the country closer to the true meaning of the words written above the entrance to the Supreme Court: Equal justice under the law.

Judge Sonia Sotomayor became the third woman to ever serve on the Supreme Court. Perhaps even more significantly, she is the first person of Hispanic heritage to ever do the job.

When the news of her nomination became public, and as she prepared herself for the lengthy process of Senate confirmation hearings, Sonia said: "I hope that as the Senate and American people learn more about me, they will see that I am an ordinary person who has been blessed with opportunities and experiences." She explained that although she had grown up in very modest and challenging circumstances, "I consider my life to be immeasurably rich."

Weeks later, at two formal ceremonies on August 8, 2009, Sonia was officially sworn in. She became a judge on the Supreme Court. It was then she knew that she'd finally made it.

What Is the American Dream?

In the 1930s, American writer James Truslow Adams was the first to talk about the American Dream. It's the idea that, in the United States, all citizens can and should be able to achieve as rewarding a life as they want. The Declaration of Independence states that "all men are created equal." This is an important concept in the American Dream. So, too, is the fact that "life, liberty and the pursuit of happiness" are considered fundamental human rights. Adams wrote that all people living in the United States of America should be able to realize their highest potential regardless of their position or class at birth.

Ever since Adams first coined the phrase, people around the world have agreed that America seems to be a special place. Sometimes it's called the land of opportunity. Many people believe that only in America is it possible to rise above one's birth circumstances and become rich, famous, or otherwise influential.

In recent years, however, some people have criticized the American Dream for raising society's expectations too high. They say it's actually not possible for every single American to have, for example, a great job, own a car, and own a house with a "white picket fence." Difficult social problems persist, like racism, poverty, gang politics, and the lack of access to a quality education. It's harder than it looks for people who are caught up in these kinds of limitations to break free and actually achieve the full, rich life that Adams was referring to.

Not bad for a Puerto Rican kid who'd grown up in the housing projects of the East Bronx, New York.

First Hispanic on the Supreme Court

When he spoke about choosing Sonia for the Supreme Court, President Obama said he considered empathy to be an important characteristic. He thought Sonia could bring this quality to the job before her. That wasn't the only quality that made Sonia appealing as a top candidate for the job. Hardworking, dedicated, and ambitious, she had proven her chops during her years at university, while she worked in private legal practice, and during her 17 years on the judge's bench.

With her confirmation in August 2009, Judge Sonia Sotomayor became the third woman to ever serve on the Supreme Court. Perhaps even more significantly, she is the first person of Hispanic heritage to ever do the job.

Hispanic and Latino: Is There a Difference?

Over 15 percent of the U.S. population consists of people of *Latino* or *Hispanic* origin. That's about 47 million people! Among the most common of this group in the United States are people of Mexican, Puerto Rican, Cuban, Colombian, Dominican, and Salvadoran origin, as well as people whose roots extend directly to Spain.

Usually, the term *Hispanic* is used to describe people living in the United States whose origins are in Spain or the Spanish-speaking countries of Latin-America. Narrowed down, the terms *Latino* and *Latina* may include people of non-Spanish-speaking Latin-American origin. Usually, these people are from Brazil, where Portuguese is spoken. Portuguese and Spanish both developed on the Iberian Peninsula in Europe, in Portugal and Spain respectively, their countries of origin.

There is little agreement about which term—*Latino* or *Hispanic*—is preferred by people who belong to this group. Both terms are used often. The term *Hispanic* implies a connection to Spain or Spanish, but many people—such as those with roots in Brazil—have no such connection. Thus, they may prefer to be called Latinos. Indeed, *Latino* seems to be an increasingly common term. It has been gaining popularity in recent years.

Mexican-Americans form more than half of all Hispanics and Latinos in the United States. More than 30 million Americans claim Mexican heritage in the United States! People of Mexican descent will sometimes identify themselves as *Chicano/Chicana*. *Chicano* is a relatively recent term that sprang up in the 1930s, when Mexicans were brought into the United States to work in the agricultural fields of California and nearby states. Originally, the word *chicano* was used as an insult. Nowadays, some Mexican-Americans dislike the term. They avoid it because it was linked with the labor strikes by Mexican farm workers in the 1960s. They feel it has negative associations. They prefer the more mainstream term *Hispanic*.

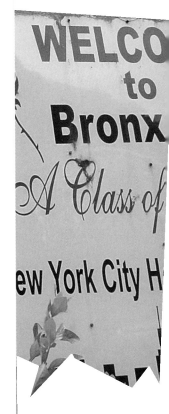

Puerto Ricans: A Unique American Group

Puerto Ricans are the second-largest group of Latinos in the United States after people of Mexican descent. Puerto Rico is a territory of the United States that was taken away from Spanish control in 1898 during the Spanish-American War. In 1917, Puerto Ricans were made U.S. citizens. Finding their opportunities on this little Caribbean island limited, many Puerto Ricans relocated to the continental United States around the 1950s. Like other groups coming to the States, they were seeking a better life for themselves.

The vast majority of these new arrivals settled in New York. Before long, they had formed the largest Hispanic ethnic group that the country had ever known. They looked different than whites, they spoke a different language, and they did things differently than other New Yorkers. Instead of being accepted into the mainstream culture, Puerto Ricans were sidelined by the dominant white cultural group.

Racism was a big problem, as it is now. Experts in Puerto Rican history say that these early Puerto Rican arrivals bore the brunt of the country's racism toward Hispanic groups. It's a bias that still exists today. Compared to other Hispanic groups in mainstream America, poverty and unemployment continue to affect Puerto Ricans more than other ethnic groups.

VOTING POWER

Latino or Hispanic—it doesn't matter which term you choose when you're looking at the vote. Every year, the number of Hispanic voters grows, and members of the government are waking up to this fact. As a group, Hispanics form a large segment of the U.S. population. They have a big voice! It would be a mistake to overlook the political power of such a large group.

Don't Go Changing

"He asked me to make him two promises," Sonia said when she reflected on her phone call with President Obama. "The first was that I remain the person I was, and the second was to stay connected to my community." When he said these words, Sonia replied that those were two things she couldn't even change if she wanted to. They were just a part of who she is.

As other Justices look on, President Barack Obama congratulates Justice Sonia Sotomayor prior to the ceremony formally admitting her onto the Supreme Court.

Chapter 2
Reading Nancy Drew in the Projects

Sonia Sotomayor was born in the Bronx, in New York City, on June 25, 1954. She, along with others of similar background, refers to herself as "Nuyorican"—a cross between a New Yorker and a Puerto Rican. Like so many other Puerto Ricans at the time, her parents had moved from their familiar island home to New York in the 1940s, during World War II. At 17, Sonia's mother Celina signed up to participate in the war effort, an act that brought her to the U.S. mainland. She moved from Puerto Rico to Georgia for her training. She was living away from her family for the first time.

Heartache and Hard Work

Sonia's father, Juan, had a third-grade education and worked in a factory as a tool and die maker. At the age of 42, he died of the very heart problems that had prevented him from being permitted to fight in the war overseas. Sonia was nine when her father passed away. In order to support Sonia and her younger brother, also named Juan, Celina ramped up her work schedule to six days a week.

Initially, Celina worked as a telephone operator at a small hospital in the South Bronx. Later, she trained to get her practical nurse's license and worked as a nurse at a drug clinic. She encouraged her children to do well in school and maintained high expectations of them. Celina Sotomayor's hard work and encouragement paid off. Sonia made it to the Supreme Court, and Juan is now a doctor and university professor living near Syracuse, New York.

Big Dreams in the Bronx

Sonia was brought up to believe she could do or be anything she wanted. Growing up in the Bronx, surrounded by other visible minorities, she didn't feel she was limited to what she could do. She didn't realize that people outside her neighborhood felt differently. It wasn't until later, when she entered the wider world of college, that she realized the truth. Until then, she hadn't known racism existed. As a kid growing up in an ethnically mixed

Sonia was brought up to believe she could do or be anything she wanted.

Sonia Sotomayor is shown with her mother Celina Sotomayor and father Juan Luis Sotomayor in this undated family photograph.

neighborhood, Sonia hadn't experienced discrimination. Out in the wide world, she realized reaching her dreams wouldn't be an easy road to travel.

Sonia and her brother were raised in the Bronx housing projects. They shared their neighborhood with people of different races and ethnic backgrounds. Most of the families were working class, just like the Sotomayors. Her home, an apartment near the elevated tracks in the Bronx, was just a few miles away from Yankee Stadium, and she grew up loving baseball and the Yankees. Sonia says she often spent her Saturday afternoons at the movies, watching comedies with her aunt and cousins. "Being a Latina child was watching the adults playing dominos on Saturday night and us kids playing loteria, bingo, with my grandmother calling out the numbers which we marked on our cards with chick peas," she once told a group of law students. It was a time of warmth, love, and good memories.

A New Challenge

When Sonia was young, one of her favorite things to do was read. Her pick for how to pass a few quiet hours? Devouring books in the Nancy Drew series. Sonia says she was a child with big dreams and was inspired by the exciting line of work pursued by the fictional red-haired detective. Sonia herself had visions of doing police and detective work when she grew up.

All those dreams were shattered when, at the age of eight, she was diagnosed with type 1 diabetes. In type 1 diabetes, the pancreas doesn't

A family of immigrants from Puerto Rico are shown in 1947. Many families left Puerto Rico for the U.S. mainland in the 1940s to join the war effort and, later, to seek out employment in the post-war economy.

Sonia's parents met when they were both living in the United States. Celina met her husband after she was discharged from the Women's Army Corps. They discovered that each of them had the same idea: to come to mainland America because they wanted to escape the grinding poverty back home. Both of them had hoped to create a better life for themselves, but especially for their children. And, as it turned out, they did.

June 1953: Families on a street in a New York neighborhood where many Puerto Ricans, Mexicans, Cubans, and other Latin Americans lived.

"We sacrificed ourselves so our children would get an education and get ahead," said Lucy Medina, a Puerto Rican woman who, like Celina, had also arrived in New York in the 1950s, hoping for a better life for her children. "A lot of women here have done that. We stayed on top of our children and made sure they didn't get sidetracked."

HOPING FOR A BETTER LIFE

produce insulin, a hormone that's responsible for converting sugar into energy. Type 1 diabetes can cause heart disease, high blood pressure, kidney problems, and even blindness or amputation. Patients with diabetes must carefully check their blood sugar levels. That tells them how much sugar is in their blood. They must give themselves insulin injections several times a day. These injections help even out the level of sugar in the blood. In recent years, automatic pumps have made it easier for diabetics to manage their blood sugar levels.

Sonia was told that detective work wouldn't be a reasonable career to pursue due to her diabetes. Sonia was disappointed, but she wasn't discouraged. She knew there would be another way for her to live an exciting life and make a difference in the world.

I Want to Be a Judge!

When Sonia's father died, she spoke mainly Spanish at home. Although English was the language of the wider U.S. culture, she couldn't speak it very well. That's when she decided to take the bull by the horns and master her second language. Sonia strengthened her English by reading as much as she could.

Sonia read a lot, but she liked watching TV, too. One of her favorite shows was Perry Mason. The popular show depicted a fictional defense attorney who made a living trying to help his clients, most of whom had been

Life in the Projects

At first, Sonia lived with her mother and brother in the Bronxdale Houses, a group of 28 seven-story buildings. It was home to people of many different ethnic and racial backgrounds. It's a rough area now, with a high level of drug-related crimes. Back when Sonia was a kid, however, the apartments were newly built, and it was a pretty safe place to be.

There was a great deal of poverty among her neighbors. Many of the people living in the area were people who worked hard for not much money, like Sonia's own mother. They were called the working poor.

Still others lived in complete poverty. Living in such conditions meant there was a lot of sickness and addiction. Sonia grew up very aware of the problems other families faced. She didn't want that to be a part of her life, either then or in the future.

Celina believed a good education was a valuable thing. She worked hard to purchase an *Encyclopaedia Britannica* for her children. No one else in the neighborhood had that!

accused of murder. All those hours of watching Perry Mason helped Sonia make an important connection. One particular episode, in which the show ended with the camera fixed on the judge, is cemented in her memory. With total clarity, it dawned on her that the judge was the person with the most power in the whole courtroom. An idea started to take shape in her young mind.

She had also noticed that Perry Mason got to do a lot of the same kinds of investigative work that she enjoyed reading about in her Nancy Drew books. So—before she had even reached the age of ten—Sonia Sotomayor of the South Bronx housing projects decided to become a lawyer. It would be her first step toward the goal of sitting behind the bench. "Once I focused on becoming a lawyer, I never deviated from that goal," she said.

An "A" Student

Sonia was a hardworking student. Her mother, feeling that the public schools in the neighborhood were too rough and dangerous, chose to send her children to Catholic schools instead. Sonia was well liked among her friends, and she graduated valedictorian at

With total clarity, it dawned on her that the judge was the person with the most power in the whole courtroom.

At school, Sonia was known for her clear thinking and her willingness to include all sorts of people in her circle of friends.

Blessed Sacrament, her South Bronx elementary school. During her high school vacations Sonia worked at a retail store, and later with her mother at Prospect Hospital.

Over time, the projects became harder edged. Crime and drugs moved in. The police came often. Sometimes they had to lock down the building in which the Sotomayors lived. In 1970, Sonia, her mother, and her younger brother moved to Co-op City in the northeast Bronx. With 35 high-rises and seven groups of townhouses, it's the world's largest co-operative housing project, which is a group of buildings where each owner pays for a small share in the real estate. Sonia attended Cardinal Spellman High School in the northeast Bronx. The Sotomayor home in Co-op City became a gathering place for Sonia's classmates and the debate team, of which she was a member. Her mother would return home after a day of nursing and feed the

The future Judge Sonia Sotomayor is shown in a cap and gown for her eighth-grade graduation.

crowd of young intellectuals a meal of rice and beans.

A True Leader

One classmate remembers Sonia as bright, popular, and dynamic—the kind of person about whom it could be said that when she entered the room, you "felt" it. Another classmate recalls that she was always well informed. She could debate almost any topic well. She'd get into deep discussions with parents, other students, teachers, or friends.

At school, Sonia was known for her clear thinking and her willingness to include all sorts of people in her circle of friends. She would often direct conversations in the lunchroom. She and her peers would talk endlessly about social systems or problems.

The war in Vietnam—a social, military, and political controversy that involved many of their own friends—was a subject of frequent debate. It was a time of major social, political, and economic change, and Sonia's generation knew it.

Sonia was quite comfortable with the idea of speaking in front of groups of assembled people. She was chosen to be the valedictorian of her graduating class in 1972. Many of her classmates saw her as a leader. Beyond a shadow of a doubt, her high school friends understood that Sonia would somehow go on to become a factor in public life.

> "I saw her as a leader, for sure," said one of her high school classmates. "[Her qualities] were teenage attributes at the time, but they were there. All of those things that make her able to do this job, or be able to handle this pressure, it was there. It was in her from the beginning."

Honoring Celina

Who is Sonia Sotomayor's biggest inspiration? Why, her mother, of course. "I stand on the shoulders of countless people, yet there is one extraordinary person who is my life aspiration," Sonia told the audience at the announcement of her nomination to the Supreme Court. "That person is my mother, Celina Sotomayor." Sonia spoke of her mother's dedication and strong work ethic that set the example for her and her brother as they were growing up in a working-class neighborhood. "I have often said that I am all I am because of her, and I am only half the woman she is."

Celina Sotomayor cries as President Barack Obama announces that Sonia Sotomayor is the nominee to replace Supreme Court Justice David Souter. This photo was taken in the East Room of the White House on May 26, 2009.

Chapter 3
The College Years

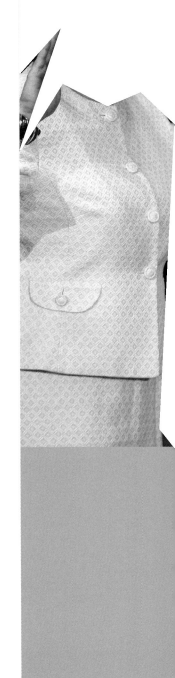

Sonia decided to pursue her studies at Princeton, an Ivy League university. Ken Moy, a friend from her high school debate team, encouraged her to join him there. Sonia decided to go. Her excellent grades meant she could attend on a full academic scholarship. Her family wouldn't have to pay any money for tuition. But Moy, who is now a lawyer in Oakland, California, warned her that attending Princeton might not be easy.

A Changing Society

Moy told Sonia that, as a Puerto Rican girl from a working-class neighborhood, she might meet some people who didn't want her there. He warned Sonia that she might be left out.

It was 1972, a time of big change in the United States. Sonia entered Princeton at a time when there were only about 20 other Latinos there. She was also arriving just a few short years after women had been grudgingly admitted to the institution. Until shortly before Sonia's arrival, women weren't wanted there. The university's alumni had strongly protested women in the lecture halls. Not only was Sonia a woman, but she was a member of a visible minority. She looked different than the other students, most of whom were white. It was a completely different situation than she had faced in high school back in the Bronx, where most of her peers were minorities. She felt like a stranger—as if she didn't belong. For the first time, Sonia felt unsure of herself.

It was an intimidating time!

College life was definitely different. Removed from her beloved home and neighborhood, Sonia lived in a dorm at the far edge of campus. She didn't belong to any of the social groups at Princeton. They were mostly white, and some of them weren't even open to women. She didn't have much in common with the prep school kids in her freshman classes, either. None of them had been raised by a single mother in one of the most poverty-stricken corners of the country, as she had.

Learning How to Write All Over Again

Sonia was too nervous and self-conscious to ask questions during most of her first year at Princeton. She was shocked to realize that despite her achievements in high school, her writing skills weren't as strong or as polished

None of them had been raised by a single mother in one of the most poverty-stricken corners of the country, as she had.

Sonia Sotomayor started her university studies in the 1970s. Back then, ethnic minorities were rare on many campuses—and that was just the way those institutions liked it, especially Ivy League schools like Yale, Harvard, and Princeton. Many religious and ethnic groups were strongly discouraged. These included Latinos, African-Americans, and Jews. Nowadays, things have changed, but many people feel some schools still limit the enrollment of certain minority groups.

Not white? Not Christian? No need to apply.

Princeton University senior Sonia Sotomayor's 1976 yearbook photo

as were those of the students who surrounded her. She was writing the way Spanish is spoken, which is very different from the way English is spoken. Her sentences were too long and complex. So she dove headlong into improving her written communication skills. She was tutored by the professor who had first pointed out the problem with her writing. She spent her spare time in the university library, where she read and worked tirelessly to improve her written skills.

At Princeton, Sonia earned a reputation as a nose-to-the-grindstone kind of student, which, of course, suited her just fine.

A New Focus: Politics

Sonia wasn't alone in feeling she didn't belong in Princeton's exclusive social scene. Other students felt that way, too. They turned their energies to politics. In a time of strong anti-war sentiment, she joined many other students and became an activist with the Third World Center on campus. She joined *Accion Puertorriqueno*, an organization that supported Puerto Rican students. It didn't take long for Sonia to find her voice again. Not long after joining the Puerto Rican student group, she became its co-chairwoman. Together, the group worked to change a college climate that discriminated against minorities. Though she had strong beliefs, Sonia was always reasonable in how she raised her opinions. She did not resort to extreme measures to make her point.

Sonia wrote letters on at least two different occasions to Princeton's president. The letters stated the group's concerns about the university's behavior. The letters charged that the university was not honoring its promise to include minority students. When these letters went unanswered, the group decided to take action. In 1974, *Accion Puertorriqueno* filed a letter of complaint with the New York office of the Federal Department of Health, Education, and Welfare. The letter claimed that the university was engaged in discrimination by not hiring staff or admitting students of Puerto Rican or Mexican ancestry. It seemed that Princeton was ignoring strict federal guidelines for including minorities. The government expected the university to include minorities among its teachers and students. Sonia's group blew the whistle on Princeton for not living up to the

She had become acutely aware of the fact that she was a visible minority. As such, she understood that the world would try to limit her success.

deal. In the end, Princeton officials promised to find ways to be more inclusive. They promised to hire minority staff and enroll more minority students. Eventually, classes dealing with Puerto Rican politics and history were also offered.

Blazing a Trail at Princeton

During her time at Princeton, Sonia served on various boards and committees. She worked as a translator for Puerto Rican and other Spanish-speaking patients at a nearby state psychiatric hospital. Many people on campus knew her personally—and if they didn't, they certainly knew of her.

Sonia majored in history. Her thesis—the most important essay she wrote as a part of her studies at Princeton—was about how Puerto Rico has struggled to develop its own political and economic systems. She was a top student and had many political achievements to her credit. She was awarded Princeton University's top award—the M. Taylor Pyne Honor Prize. She graduated summa cum laude—the highest academic distinction—from Princeton in 1976. During her time there, Sonia had grown a lot. She had developed her speaking skills even more. She read widely, had excellent thinking skills, and wasn't afraid to help others if she believed in their cause. She had become acutely aware of the fact that she was a visible minority. As such, she understood that the world would try to limit her success. At Princeton, she had

Opposite: This photo of Sonia Sotomayor was taken around the time she won the M. Taylor Pyne Honor Prize at Princeton University.

On August 14, 1976, after she graduated from Princeton, Sonia married her high school sweetheart, Kevin Noonan. She changed her surname to Sotomayor de Noonan. Kevin was a biologist in his early career, and then he moved on to become a biotech patent lawyer. The pair divorced in 1983. By all accounts—including friends, family, and Noonan himself—the divorce was friendly.

In 1998, when Sonia was inducted into the United States Court of Appeals, she was engaged to New York construction contractor Peter White. The wedding bells never rang for this union, however; they split just two years later.

Today, Sonia remains unmarried, possibly because her job demands so much of her time. The judge herself has mentioned how she has elected to remain single and without children in pursuit of a professional career. She admits that loneliness is a faithful companion.

Once Married, Once Engaged, Often Lonely

faced racism and fought prejudice. She became a stronger person as a result. Sonia had learned to draw strength from her identity as a Latina.

For Sonia, her time at Princeton had been a life-changing experience.

Sonia wanted to be a lawyer. It was the perfect fit for the thoughtful young woman.

The Yale Years

In the fall of 1976, Sonia returned to the classroom. She was on another full scholarship, this time at Yale University, in New Haven, Connecticut. At Yale, Sonia was as busy and involved as ever. She became an editor of the Yale Law Journal and was managing editor of another student-run journal, one devoted to international law.

Again, Sonia found herself one of only a handful of Latino students. She became involved in various advocacy initiatives, including fighting to have more Hispanic faculty hired by the esteemed university.

She proved herself a gifted and tolerant debater who was able to state the positions of opposing sides in clear, fair terms. She was co-chair of a group representing the interests

THE FIRST VICTORY IS THE SWEETEST

In her third year at Yale, Sonia filed a formal complaint against an important law firm in Washington, D.C. She had gone to a recruiting dinner with Shaw, Pittman, Potts & Trowbridge. They were looking for new young lawyers to join them at the firm. Sometime during the meal, it was suggested that Sonia was only at Yale due to affirmative action, a program that favors those who may have suffered some form of discrimination, particularly in employment or education. Sonia was furious. She turned down further interview opportunities with the firm. Instead, she filed a complaint with a faculty-student committee. The committee decided that Sonia's complaint was fair. A debate raged across campus about the complaint she had filed. In the end, the firm formally apologized. This fact was reported publicly in the pages of the Washington Post.

of Native-American, Asian, and Latino students. Her friends at the time often thought she seemed older than her real age. They chalked it up to Sonia having to battle her way out of a disadvantaged childhood.

Sonia liked being everyone's friend. Her classmates remembered that she would gravitate to the workers, the janitors, and the everyday people in the cafeteria. Sonia included everyone and accepted all for who they were. Banding together with other minority students, she had as her closest friends at Yale a Mexican-American, a Puerto Rican, a Mohawk Indian, and an African-American. In their free time, the group would get together to watch baseball at one another's apartments or head to a local club and dance the night away.

Fun and games aside, Sonia knew exactly what she wanted when she graduated. She wanted to be a lawyer. It was the perfect fit for the thoughtful young woman. She was "tough, clear, very quick on her feet," said Martha Minnow, one of Sonia's friends who went on to be a Harvard Law School professor.

Sonia graduated from Yale with her law degree, called a J.D. or Juris Doctor, in 1979. She was 25.

"I chose to be a lawyer and ultimately a judge because I find endless challenge in the complexities of the law, I firmly believe in the rule of law as the foundation for all of our basic rights."

Sonia Sotomayor

What Does a Lawyer Do?

The law is the system of rules that a government develops and puts in writing. These rules are meant to keep order and stability within the society. The law determines how criminal activity will be punished and how victims will be compensated.

Another name for a lawyer is an attorney. Many lawyers do their work inside a courtroom, presenting arguments to a judge or sometimes a judge and jury (as shown in the photo, right). These are called trial lawyers.

Some lawyers don't go to court at all. Instead, they do only the legal work that can be done outside the courts—things like drawing up wills and real estate contracts.

To be a lawyer you need to go to law school. Usually you have to have a four-year undergraduate degree first, before you can do your three-year law degree. Law school is where students learn the ins and outs of the laws—how to read them, how to explain the laws to their clients, and how to present a case to a jury and a judge. A lawyer's job is to advocate, or speak out, on behalf of his or her clients and to seek the best possible outcome that the law will permit.

Law schools in the United States grant two kinds of degrees. A Master of Laws (LL.M.) is an advanced academic degree.

A Juris Doctor (J.D.) is a professional degree required to practice law. This is a different degree than the Bachelor of Laws (LL.B.), which is necessary to be an attorney in most other parts of the world where common law is practiced.

Chapter 4
Law and Order on the Streets of New York

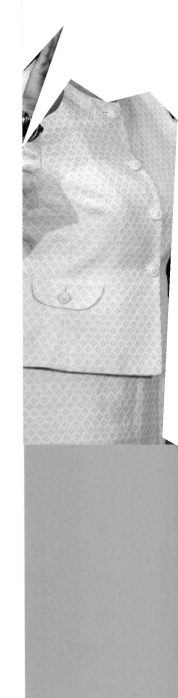

When Sonia graduated from law school, one of her professors recommended her to a friend of his, Manhattan District Attorney Robert Morgenthau. In 1979, she took a job as an assistant district attorney at Morgenthau's office. She was back on her beloved New York soil!

A Workaholic Is Born

The city had changed in the time Sonia was away at college. Crime was spiraling out of control, and drug problems were rampant across the region. On average, New York was experiencing 1,800 murders a year—that's three times the rate today.

Sonia had heard all about the heavy caseload for D.A. Robert Morgenthau's staff, too. On top of it all, she was nervous about appearing in court in front of judges.

Despite her concerns, she packed her bags and set up house in an Italian neighborhood in Brooklyn. She brought her typical zeal to the job, working 15-hour days to prosecute crimes like shoplifting, robberies, assaults, murder, and child pornography. She wasn't afraid to go out and interview witnesses in some of the more rundown parts of town. She also gained confidence in working with judges.

It was a busy time. Sonia left for work at 7:00 a.m. and would often return later than 10:00 p.m. Her husband was away at graduate school in New Jersey. She sometimes did legal consulting for friends and family from her home office in Brooklyn. She worked hard and built a reputation as being prepared, fair, and effective, but the job eventually burned her out and made her sad. "After a while, you forget that there are decent, law-abiding people in the world," Sonia said.

Private Practice

In 1984, Sonia accepted a position with Pavia & Harcourt in Manhattan, a small commercial law firm. Having been told by the district attorney's office that Sonia was a "potential

Sonia brought her typical zeal to the job, working 15-hour days to prosecute crimes like shoplifting, robberies, assaults, murder, and child pornography.

"Some of the judges like to push around young assistants and get them to dispose of cases. Well, no one pushed around Sonia Sotomayor; she stood up to the judges, in an appropriate way."

Manhattan District Attorney Robert Morganthau

In this photo, a man looks into the window of a bar in which two men had been shot to death and several others seriously wounded. Such shootings and other forms of violence had become increasingly common in New York by the time Sonia Sotomayor returned to the city in 1979 to work as a prosecuting attorney.

superstar," the firm was glad to have her on board. She worked with 29 other lawyers in intellectual property, international law, and arbitration.

For Sonia, it was a break from the felonies she had been prosecuting at the D.A.'s office. Her salary increased. She spent her time representing international companies that did business in the United States. At Pavia & Harcourt, her main work was to try cases against Fendi counterfeiters—the people who make knock-off handbags and jewelry using the famous designer's insignia.

The workload at Pavia & Harcourt was lighter than it was at the D.A.'s office. Sonia, however, continued to live her life with an intense energy. In 1987, the governor of the State of New York appointed Sonia to the Board of the State of New York Mortgage Agency. She held this unpaid position for a total of five years, helping low-income people get loans to purchase homes. Sonia was widely admired by board members as being fair and for helping give a voice to people who otherwise weren't very well represented.

Having been told by the district attorney's office that Sonia was a "potential superstar," Pavia & Harcourt was glad to have her on board.

Sonia the Brave

As both a prosecuting attorney and a lawyer working for a private firm, Sonia was known for her compassion and her courage.

Once, while staying at a friend's apartment during a busy trial, Sonia returned to find the place had been burglarized. Sonia had grown up in the Bronx—and her friend had grown up in Queens—and the two were completely unfazed by the break-in.

Sometimes Sonia's job at the firm of Pavia & Harcourt involved following tips provided by the U.S. border control agency. Sonia would have to go out to a fashion counterfeiter's warehouse and help seize suspicious merchandise. One time, on a case that saw her investigating Chinese counterfeiters, Sonia wore a bulletproof vest to her lunch date in Chinatown. Once—with that Bronx-born Sotomayor determination—she even hopped on a motorcycle and chased after a fleeing counterfeiter through the streets of New York!

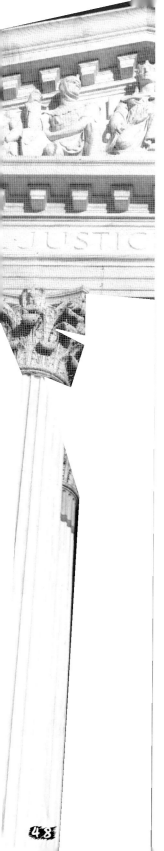

Sonia was a vocal advocate for the right to affordable housing. Over the years, she also served on a variety of other boards, including the New York City Campaign Finance Board, the Board of the Puerto Rican Legal Defense and Education Fund, and the Board of the Maternity Center Association.

When Making Partner Makes You Miserable

In 1988, Sonia became a partner at Pavia & Harcourt. Lawyers usually love the idea of becoming a partner in a law firm. It means more money, more prestige, and better cases. By that time, however, this kind of work had become less rewarding for Sonia. It didn't bring her much satisfaction. Sonia had had brighter dreams for herself in college. "The vast majority of lawyering is drudgery work," she said in a 1986 television interview. "It's sitting in a library, it's banging out a brief, it's talking to clients for endless hours." It was time for a change. Sonia wanted to go back to doing what she did best—working more directly on behalf of others.

What Does a Board do?

A board of directors is a group of elected or appointed people. They work together to supervise the activity of a company or organization. They're not the actual people who run the organization; rather, they are more like their supervisors. Boards are made up of all different types of people. The more diverse the board, the more balanced it tends to be. Sometimes it might be called a board of trustees, a board of governors, or a board of managers. Whatever its formal name, the essential job of a board remains the same:

- to select the person who runs the organization (that's the Chief Executive Officer, or CEO);
- to make sure there's enough money to run the organization and to oversee how much money will be spent by the organization in its work;
- to oversee and govern the organization by creating rules and goals; and
- to report back to the people who care (sometimes investors) about how the organization is doing its job.

Often, a board member's work is unpaid. Often his or her work experience is valuable to the organization. The unpaid work done by such a person is a community service—a way for an individual to give back to his or her community by lending a bit of time and guidance.

Chapter 5
On the Bench at Last

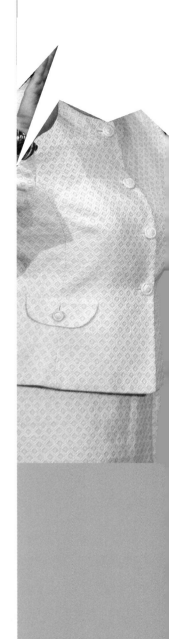

Ever since elementary school, Sonia had wanted to be a judge. After 13 years of being a lawyer, her time finally arrived. In 1991, New York's Democratic U.S. Senator Daniel Patrick Moynihan recommended Sonia to the bench.

A Promise Fulfilled

Moynihan was pleased to suggest Sonia for the position because he shared a personal understanding of her circumstances. Moynihan was an Irish American who grew up in a poor neighborhood. Like Sonia, he came from a working-class background, and he knew about the challenges in trying to rise out of poverty and oppression to create a successful career.

Moynihan had also made a promise to get a Hispanic judge appointed for the state of New York, and Sonia was a perfect candidate. He hoped and believed that one day, Sonia might also become the first Hispanic Supreme Court justice.

On November 27, 1991, Sonia was nominated by the first President George Bush to a seat on the U.S. District Court for the Southern District of New York. She was confirmed in 1992 by unanimous consent of the Senate Judiciary Committee. Still in her 30s, Sonia was the youngest judge in the Southern District. She was also the first Hispanic federal judge in the state of New York, and the first Puerto Rican woman to serve as a judge in a U.S. federal court. At the time, there were seven women among the 58 judges in her district.

Less Cash, Better Job

Being promoted to judge was a great career step for Sonia, but there was another side to Sonia's acceptance of this new position. Every lawyer knows that the way to get rich quick is in running a private law practice, but Sonia wasn't in it to become as wealthy as possible. She knew that turning her back on private practice would mean she'd never earn as much money as some of her peers. Sure, she would receive a salary as a judge, but since it was paid with public funds from taxpayers' money, it wasn't going to be huge.

When she left Pavia & Harcourt, she said, "I've never wanted to get adjusted to my income because I knew I wanted to go back to public service." Besides, she said, compared to

Sonia Sotomayor was the first Puerto Rican woman to serve as a judge in a U.S. federal court.

what her own mother was earning at the time—and compared to the humble way in which she had been raised—it didn't really qualify as a "modest" salary.

Sonia was able to bolster her judicial earnings with a bit of income from teaching at the law schools of New York University and Columbia University, both in New York.

Sonia packed her bags—again—and moved back to the Bronx so she could live within her judicial district. Being a judge was a big departure from being a lawyer. From now on, her life would be busier—and lonelier. "We are more isolated than at a law firm," said Judge Miriam Goldman Cedarbaum, who became a friend of Sonia's. "You still have good friendships, but it's a different world." Gone were the days of easy socializing at the law firm. Sonia told her friends she wasn't going to be dating lawyers any more, either. She had drawn her social circle that little bit tighter.

> *"When you don't have money, it's easy. There isn't anything there to report."*
>
> Sonia Sotomayor, on filling out forms reporting your income when you are making a judge's salary

Female Judges Are Rare

There aren't very many female judges in the United States. Even though women sit on the highest courts in nearly all of the U.S. states and territories—including Puerto Rico—their numbers are small. As of 2008, about one-quarter of the federal judiciary was made up of women. That's counting Supreme Court, Circuit Court, and District Court judges.

Back in 1992, when Sonia Sotomayor was first appointed as a District Court Judge, the figure was only 13 percent. At present, only two of the nine Supreme Court justices are women.

Currently, female students make up roughly half of all law school classes in the United States. Among the practicing lawyers in the United States, one-third of them are women. With only about 25 percent of the federal judiciary being made up of women, it seems that the higher women climb in the legal profession, the fewer there are.

A Strong and Thoughtful Judge

Wearing robes for the first time ever, Sonia went to work in a federal district courthouse in New York City. She heard cases that dealt with fraud and other kinds of financial crimes, such as embezzlement, identity theft, and forgery. In her new role, Sonia showed herself to be a strong judge. She wasn't about to let anybody intimidate her into ruling in a way that wasn't faithful to the law. She wasn't afraid to rule against the government. She gained a reputation for handing out tough sentences, based on "just the facts," as her mentor and friend Judge Cedarbaum suggested she do. Sonia prepared herself well by studying her cases thoroughly, and she didn't allow any time to be wasted in the courtroom.

Case Closed

Between 1992 and 1998, when she moved on to the Court of Appeals for the Second Circuit, Sonia heard about 450 cases. Here's a brief look at some of the cases that came before Judge Sonia Sotomayor while she was a District Court judge:

- In 1993 Sonia declared a law unconstitutional that prohibited a Hanukkah menorah from being displayed in a public park.
- In 1994 Sonia ordered prison officials in New York to let inmates tuck beads under their belts in honor of the Santeria religion, despite the officials' protests that the beads were gang symbols. She said the prison officials were too biased toward the mainstream Christian religion in not allowing the inmates to wear the beads of this little-known faith.
- In 1998 she ruled that the jobless and homeless people hired by three nonprofit agencies in New York had to earn minimum wage when working for these agencies. The agencies had been paying the workers less than minimum wage on the claim that they were not employees, but simply trainees.

The case for which Sonia Sotomayor is perhaps best known came in 1995, when she single-handedly brought a long national baseball strike to an end. Baseball team owners had wanted to change the rules around player salaries and other issues by forcing a new contract on the players. The players didn't like the new agreement, and so they went on strike. The strike lasted long enough that the 1994 World Series was canceled! Eventually, the case came before Judge Sotomayor. Just

Some judges tend toward making very broad statements when they hand down their rulings. Not Sonia. As a federal judge, she stuck to the facts and kept her eye on the real issue. That's not to say her decisions weren't lengthy—often they were! But they reflected a tendency to make narrow rulings that were focused in on the problem at hand.

A Bulldog on the Bench?

Early in her career as a judge, Sonia became known by lawyers and judges alike as intelligent and direct. Her critics said she could be sharp and curt toward lawyers. Indeed, she subjected lawyers to thorough and vigorous questioning. Straightforward to the point of being blunt, Judge Sotomayor showed little patience for lawyers who came into her courtroom without being adequately prepared.

one day before the new baseball season was scheduled to begin, she ruled in favor of the players, saying that the owners weren't upholding fair labor process.

Major league baseball resumed. For a while after her decision, Sonia Sotomayor was known as one of baseball's saviors, and she was widely celebrated in cities with major league teams.

One notable journalist wrote that, in saving the season, Judge Sotomayor had risen to join the ranks of such baseball greats as Joe DiMaggio, Willie Mays, Jackie Robinson, and Ted Williams! (Insiders say it took Sonia a grand total of 15 minutes to weigh the case before she made her decision!)

Opposit: On April 27, 1995, Milwaukee Brewers left fielder Turner Ward loosens up between innings in a game against the White Sox at Comiskey Park in Chicago. The game is the season home opener for the White Sox, and fans sitting among empty bleacher seats display a sign showing their opinion of the recent baseball strike. One day before the start of the 1995 season, Sonia Sotomayor issued a ruling that "saved" the 1995 season.

Chapter 6
Life as a Judge in the Court of Appeals

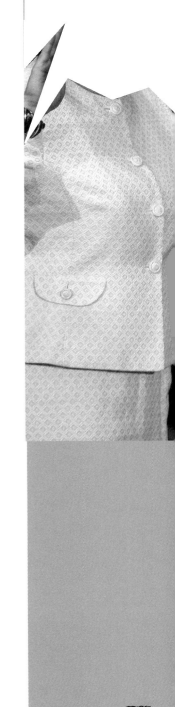

Sonia's next big career shakeup came in June 1997, when President Bill Clinton nominated her to a seat on the U.S. Court of Appeals for the Second Circuit. Located in Manhattan, this is one of 13 United States Courts of Appeals. Its territory includes Vermont, Connecticut, and New York state, and it's known as one of the country's most demanding circuits. The appellate court's job? To listen to the cases that are appealed, or passed along, from the lower, District Courts.

On the Fast Track to the Supreme Court?

The American Bar Association supervises all legal practice in the United States. It had given Sonia a thumbs-up for a position on the bench. It issued a statement saying she was "well qualified" for the spot. The nomination was thrilling for Sonia, but it came with a few bumps, too. Critics—mostly Republican senators—accused Sonia of being way too liberal. Republicans tend to be more conservative people who value home and family, often over more typically liberal ideals like equality and freedom.

Indeed, many of the decisions Sonia had made at the district court showed her liberal leanings, especially those involving free speech or cases where employers weren't fair to their workers. Judges are labeled as liberals or conservatives all the time. For the most part, many legal experts consider Sonia to be in the middle of the liberal-conservative spectrum.

Still, Republicans delayed the vote for as long as they could, saying that President Clinton was trying to fast-track Sonia to the Supreme Court. Things were looking grim. Eventually, Republican Senator Alfonse M. D'Amato pressured the Senate leadership to vote on Sonia's nomination. Several Hispanic organizations in his home district of New York state were tired of waiting. They asked him to try to move the process along. They said the Senate was just stalling. D'Amato liked Sonia, and he supported her nomination. So he asked the Senate to make a decision about her nomination. Besides, he was up for re-election that year—and he needed the Hispanic vote!

Sonia felt bitter. She felt that the Senate Judiciary Committee had stereotyped her, assuming they understood her political beliefs based on the fact that she was a Latina.

The White House, Up Close and Personal

As part of the nomination and confirmation process for Sonia's promotion to the U.S. Court of Appeals for the Second Circuit, Sonia was given a private tour of the White House. It was an amazing experience for her. As she thought back to her childhood and all the experience she had had that brought her to this point in her career, she said: "I felt I was on top of the world. And I was."

Finally, on October 2, 1998, Sonia was confirmed to the Second Circuit bench. A process that originally was supposed to simply have been rubber-stamped had actually taken more than a year.

In the wake of the experience, Sonia felt bitter. She felt that the Senate Judicial Committee at the time had stereotyped her, assuming they understood her political beliefs based on the fact that she was a Latina. She felt they were judging her more on who she seemed to be, rather than the nature of the cases she ruled on.

> "[T]he aspiration to impartiality is just that—it's an aspiration because it denies the fact that we are by our experiences making different choices than others."
>
> Sonia Sotomayor

Does Being a Latina Make Sonia a Different Kind of Judge?

Sonia has done a lot of thinking about how personal experiences affect the way she makes up her mind in cases. She understands that people have different experiences in life, and because of that, people approach issues differently based on their personal life experience. She has said that "the aspiration to impartiality is just that—it's an aspiration because it denies the fact that we are by our experiences making different choices than others." It's hard to be impartial. There probably aren't very many judges in the world who would disagree.

In a 2001 address to the graduating law class at the University of California at Berkeley, Sonia talked about how her own personal experiences have shaped her as a person—and as a judge. She said that each day she works on the bench, she learns new things about being a judge. She is always learning new things about what it means to be a professional Latina in a world of prejudice. In her speech, Sonia recognized that she's human. She, like other judges, tries to do her best to not let her own experience and history affect her judgment too much.

A "Wise Latina" Sparks Debate

During the same address at the University of California at Berkeley, Sonia made a comment that her critics have never let her forget. She acknowledged that most of the important decisions about sex and race discrimination cases have been made by just such a group. Sonia said, "I would hope that a wise Latina woman with the richness of her experience would more often than not reach a better conclusion than a white male who hasn't lived that life." At Berkeley, the comment didn't raise anyone's eyebrows. It was part of a much longer speech. The speech was a thoughtful reflection of how real life shapes a judge's approach to the job. But Sonia's critics seized on her words. They took the "wise Latina" comment and said she was a racist. One judge thundered that if he had ever made such a comment during his career, he'd have been fired. Sonia's supporters say the quote was taken out of context.

Sonia's critics are also quick to note that she has a history of activism. They point to her politically charged days at Princeton. Back then, she advocated on behalf of Puerto Rican students. But her student activism was always measured and calm. She wasn't a foaming-at-the-mouth radical, as her critics tried to make the public believe.

Sonia's supporters say her natural tendency to sympathize with minorities does not seem to affect her rulings. She regularly rejects cases dealing with racial discrimination. Was it a personal agenda of activism? Or was it a willingness to examine each case carefully and apply the law as it is written?

Sonia's critics seized on her words. They took the 'wise Latina' comment and said she was a racist.

Taking No Decision Lightly

Sonia was always very careful to practice law in the fairest manner possible. She never lost sight of the fact that her decisions could—indeed, would—change lives. "Judges must be extraordinarily sensitive to the impact of their

She never lost sight of the fact that her decisions could—indeed, would—change lives.

decisions and function within, and respectful of, the Constitution," she once wrote. She never forgot that the cases she heard were about real people with real problems. The worlds of these real people were seriously disrupted by these court cases.

Sonia experienced a lot growing up in the Bronx. As a judge, she says her personal and professional experiences helped her understand the cases that come before her:

"It has helped me to understand, respect, and respond to the concerns and arguments of all litigants who appear before me, as well as to the views of my colleagues on the bench. I strive never to forget the real-world consequences of my decisions on individuals, businesses, and government."

We Trust Your Judgment

Sonia's judgment is generally well regarded by other judges. As is common in the practice of law, many other judges use her rulings to help them make decisions in their own cases. Some of her most notable decisions while in this post included those dealing with child custody cases and complex business cases. Many legal experts feel Sonia has an admirably sophisticated grasp of the law. "She appreciates the complexity of issues," said Yale professor Stephen L. Carter. Professor Carter teaches some of Sonia's opinions in his classes. When she's facing a difficult case, Carter said, "she doesn't leap at its throat but reasons to get to the bottom of issues."

> *"I strive never to forget the real-world consequences of my decisions on individuals, businesses, and government."*
>
> Sonia Sotomayor

A Controversial Decision

Every now and then, a judge who is known for fair and balanced rulings makes a decision that leaves people scratching their heads. People questioned Sonia's ruling in Ricci v. DeStefano. It was a high-profile case that pitted a group of white firefighters against their employer.

One Hispanic and 19 white firefighters were angry that their employer refused to promote them. The group had scored higher on fitness tests than other minority firefighters in their unit. Not enough minority firefighters got high scores—at least not enough to satisfy the New Haven Fire Department, so they threw out the results of the tests. The group of firefighters accused the fire department of only wanting to promote non-white people.

Judge Sotomayor ruled against the white firefighters' challenge. She was one of three judges on the appeals court panel who ruled this way. Their ruling was widely criticized. Critics said the judges who heard the appeal hadn't considered all the factors in the case carefully enough. They said the decision was made hastily. They felt the one-paragraph summary that Sonia wrote was too short to properly explain such a complicated case. One

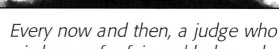

Every now and then, a judge who is known for fair and balanced rulings makes a decision that leaves people scratching their heads.

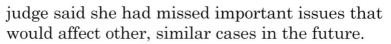

judge said she had missed important issues that would affect other, similar cases in the future.

The case went on to the Supreme Court. The Supreme Court reversed the lower court's decision by a vote of five to four. It was found that indeed, the firefighters had been victims of racial discrimination.

A Roundup of Second Circuit Cases

While serving on the Second Circuit, Sonia worked on a host of other cases that tested her sense of fairness and her understanding of the law. All of these added to the wealth of experience and credibility that led to her being considered for an appointment to the Supreme Court.

In 2001, Sonia ruled in favor of an employer that had searched its employee's computer without the employee's consent. She decided that, while employees can expect some privacy, being in a workplace usually means a diminished amount of privacy—and since the employee had been coming to work late, it was reasonable to assume that there might have been misconduct on the employee's part.

In 2002, Sonia went against the other two judges on the Second Circuit panel in deciding that an employee of the New York Police Department should not have been fired from his job even though he sent racist materials through the mail. Sonia said the man was protected by the First Amendment, which entitled him to free speech. She said that while the materials were hateful and offensive, since the man had mailed them on his own time, he couldn't be disciplined by his employer.

In 2007, Sonia ruled in favor of the environment—and against power plants. She ordered the power plants to make improvements to protect animals that live in the nearby water. She said the power plants should purchase the best technology they could afford in order to protect these aquatic organisms.

A Well-Read Jurist

Sonia spent 11 years on the Circuit Court, during which time she heard appeals in more than 3,000 cases! She was a very dedicated judge, reading all the supporting documents for cases she reviewed and writing at length about her rulings. In the span of time that she worked on the Second Circuit, Sonia wrote approximately 380 opinions.

Not Just a Judge

From 1998 to 2007, while she was working on the Second Circuit, Sonia taught law at New York University School of Law. As if that didn't fill out her busy schedule enough, she also found time to teach at Columbia Law School.

Chapter 7
Nomination to the Supreme Court: The Opportunity of a Lifetime

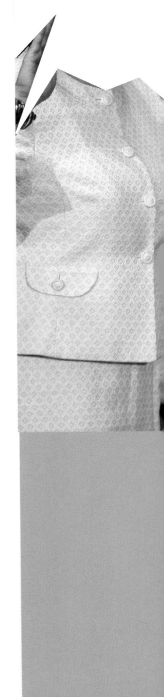

In 2005, Supreme Court Justice Sandra Day O'Connor unexpectedly announced her retirement. Two Democratic members of the Senate Judiciary Committee suggested Sonia Sotomayor to President George W. Bush. She was one of several Hispanic candidates to fill the vacancy. President Bush, who was politically conservative on most issues, decided against nominating a liberal judge during his term as president.

The Moment Is Right

Sonia's next big chance didn't come until four years later, when President Barack Obama made the move to nominate her in the spring of 2009.

George Pavia was one of Sonia's employers from her days of private law practice. He said her nomination to the Supreme Court was just like Barack Obama's rise to the presidency. It showed that the American Dream is still alive. Anybody can make it.

If It's 10:00 p.m. and Sonia's Working ... So Are Her Clerks

Sonia is a busy boss to work for. Her clerks have to be ready to jump up at a moment's notice to appear at her office doorway to answer her questions as she reviews case briefs. Sonia often asks for complete trial transcripts for cases that are being appealed. And she reads them through, cover to cover.

Sure, she's busy and has high expectations of her staff—but she's not cold or uncaring. Sonia is interested in the personal lives and careers of her clerks and has been known to treat them as family. She instructs them in how to behave in New York. She tells them to take the subway, skip the cabs, cross the bridge to eat pizza at Grimaldi's in Brooklyn Heights, and dance the salsa. She stays in touch with many of her staff as they move on

Sonia is interested in the personal lives and careers of her clerks and has been known to treat them as family.

Opposite: On May 26, 2009, President Barack Obama and Vice President Joe Biden escort Judge Sonia Sotomayor to the East Room of the White House, where the president will introduce her as his nominee for the U.S. Supreme Court.

"She [Sonia] is, in a way, a counterpart of Obama himself.... It's the American Dream—anybody can make it."

George Pavia

with their careers, keeping framed photos of them—and even of their families—in her office. "She felt like there were some rules of the game that she did not know right away and she wanted to teach us," said one woman who clerked for Sonia in 2002–2003. Once, when she interviewed another young law student, Sonia surprised him by making her first question about himself and his family, instead of kicking off the session with a question related to the legal profession, as most other judges would. One of her greatest regrets, according to some of Sonia's friends, is that she never was a law clerk herself.

The Nomination ... and the Backlash

On May 26, 2009, President Obama nominated Sonia Sotomayor to the Supreme Court. The act would make her only the second judge in U.S. history to be nominated to three different judicial posts by three different presidents.

In making his nomination, President Obama explained his interest in bringing a second woman to the Supreme Court. Three other female judges were interviewed for the position before he made his selection.

Republican senators didn't like the fact that Sonia had been nominated. Conservative groups like the National Rifle Association and pro-life organizations (groups that don't want women to have abortions) didn't like it, either. These critics pounced when the president said empathy was one of the reasons he had chosen her. They declared that empathy was a code

Throughout her career, Sonia has been known as a woman who gets along with a wide variety of people in many walks of life. Here, she shares a laugh with members of the staff of the White House Counsel's office at her birthday party on June 24, 2009, the day before her 55th birthday.

word for a liberal activist. They said she would use the law to achieve her own social ends. They thought she would be a "soft" judge who would use her power to push her own wishes for how society could be changed.

> "She has an amazing story, but she's also just an amazing person," said one man who had clerked for Sonia from 1998 to 1999. "She was the judge who, in the courthouse for example, knew all of the doormen, knew the cafeteria workers, who knew the janitors—she didn't just know all of the other judges and the politicians. She really went out of her way to get to know everyone and was well loved by everyone."

"Judge Sotomayor is a liberal judicial activist of the first order who thinks her own personal political agenda is more important than the law as written," sneered one Republican. Sonia's critics were also quick to find flaw with her crisp, impatient manner on the bench. True, Sonia's rulings do sometimes indicate a more liberal philosophy than some of the other Supreme Court justices, but none of them think she's an extreme liberal. Only her critics think so.

A Judge's Job: To Follow the Law

Sonia's three days of confirmation hearings began on July 13, 2009. During the hearings, Sonia tried to play down some of the warm comments President Obama had made about her. The word "empathy" had especially given her critics rich ammunition against her. Where he spoke at length about her "extraordinary journey" from a hardscrabble life in the Bronx to the very top of the judicial system, she re-explained. She said that her approach to being a judge was not influenced as much by her history as it was by her desire to apply the law as it is written.

Throughout the confirmation hearings, she took pains to repeat—over and over—her overall judicial philosophy of maintaining fidelity to the law. She challenged her critics' assertion that personal biases steer her rulings. She pointed to her 17 successful years on the bench, noting her job was to "apply the law to the facts at hand." She noted that, certainly, her empathy is what helps her get a handle on a given case—but that it doesn't mean she makes a ruling in order to prove a point. "My personal and professional experiences help me to listen and understand," she said to the Senate Judiciary Committee, "with the law always commanding the result in every case."

At every step along the way during her confirmation hearings, Republican senators questioned Judge Sotomayor on her stances with regard to hot-button political and social topics such as abortion and gun rights. These are

LIFE LESSONS

Margarita Rosa was a friend of Sonia's from Princeton. She shared a similar background with Sonia. Rosa also went on to pursue a career in law. She says that Sonia's experiences helped shape the person she turned out to be. "We came up in a period of time with a sense of conscience about social justice," said Rosa. "It grounded us in a set of values that told us our lives could be about something more than ourselves and the size of our bank account. That is a lesson many of us carry."

important issues for American conservatives and they're the people that the Republican party represents. Sonia had never given any major decisions concerning either of these issues, nor on other controversial topics such as the death penalty, gay rights, and national security. Her detractors had little ground to stand on.

Grace Under Fire

When she was faced with criticism about the now-famous "wise Latina" comment she had made back in 2001 to the graduating class at Berkeley, Sonia marveled that "no words I have ever spoken or written have received so much attention." She explained the statement as a comment that didn't come across the way she had wanted it to. She said it was being made into a bigger issue by her critics than it needed to be.

Sonia was grilled, quizzed, and questioned by Republican senators for hours. On several occasions she was asked the exact

President Obama watches the Senate confirmation hearings on Sonia's Supreme Court appointment on July 14, 2009.

JUDGING THE JUDGE

Before and during the confirmation hearings, people were talking about Sonia—and not always in a nice way. Talk radio, websites, and news programs across the United States were abuzz with anti-Sonia discussions. Outspoken personalities like Rush Limbaugh and Newt Gingrich said she was a racist. They picked over her public speeches and examined every detail.

Sonia's dedication and ambition were things that inspired President Obama to nominate her to the Supreme Court. At the same time, Sonia's struggles to leave behind a life of poverty and powerlessness made her a target for those who didn't want to see her on the Supreme Court. Many politicians, journalists, and legal professionals weighed in, and accused her of being unable to separate the law from her own biases and experiences with hardship.

Republican senators who opposed Sonia's nomination expressed concern over what some called her "personal bias based on ethnicity and gender." Others felt that sort of comment would never have come up had the nominee belonged to the dominant cultural group that traditionally makes up the Supreme Court: white males. Several opposing Republican senators took great pains to explain that their unwillingness to support Sonia in no way reflected anti-Hispanic sentiments. Also, none of her critics admitted anything about their opposition to her nomination being related to the fact that she's a woman.

same question, but by different senators. Each time, she listened carefully to whoever was speaking and answered with grace and composure.

On July 28, 2009, the Senate Judiciary Committee voted 13 to 6 to endorse Sonia's nomination.

Throughout the course of the confirmation hearings, she showed herself to be very well prepared and was able to speak knowledgeably on most of the cases that the senators asked her about. True to her diligent and methodical nature, Sonia had spent a lot of time preparing herself for these hearings. Through all the questions—questions that sometimes bordered on accusations —Sonia kept her cool and stayed true to her message: Regardless of a case's content or nature, the law is what tells her how to rule on it.

First created in 1816, the Senate Judiciary Committee is more formally known as The United States Senate Committee on the Judiciary. At present, the Committee is made up of 19 members, all of whom are senators. With Democrats holding a majority of seats in the Senate, most of the committee is made up of Democrats, with a minority of Republicans.

The Senate Judiciary Committee is a standing committee of the U.S. Senate, which means that although group membership may change from year to year, it is a permanent panel within the Senate.

The Senate Judiciary Committee

One of the Senate Judiciary Committee's jobs is to hold hearings before the Senate votes on whether to confirm a federal judge who has been nominated by the U.S. president.

Big Shoes to Fill

Joining the Supreme Court isn't just a matter of putting on your robe and taking out your reading glasses. For Sonia Sotomayor, as for anyone else, coming into a group of people who have worked together for years means she had to tread lightly. It was—and still is—important to figure out the other justices' personalities and the way they work together.

"The Supreme Court is an intimate group of equals who will live together for years," said Professor Richard H. Pildes, a law professor at New York University. According to Pildes, most newcomers are well advised to figure out the group dynamics before jumping in and blazing a trail for themselves.

When Sonia Sotomayor first took her seat in the Supreme Court, it was at the far end of the bench. (The chair that's farthest to the right for spectators belongs to the junior justice.) The four judges beside her seat got to shuffle down a place. It's a bit of a grunt job, this junior justice thing: it's Sonia's responsibility to serve coffee during meetings, and to communicate the court's orders to the court's clerk. When the judges have a discussion or a vote, Sonia is the last one to get to speak. And when someone knocks on the door during the group's private meetings, it's Sonia who has to get up and answer it.

The U.S. Supreme Court poses for its official portrait following the confirmation of Sonia as a member. Front row: Associate Justices Anthony M. Kennedy and John Paul Stevens; Chief Justice John G. Roberts; Associate Justices Antonin G. Scalia and Clarence Thomas. Back row: Associate Justices Samuel A. Alito, Ruth Bader Ginsburg, Stephen G. Breyer, and Sonia Sotomayor.

Judges Don't Legislate from the Bench ... Do They?

Another comment Sonia had made several years earlier came back to haunt her during the confirmation hearings. In speaking at a conference Duke University Law School in 2005, she had told the panel that the court of appeals "is where policy is made." Both Sonia

Sonia brought more federal justice experience to the Supreme Court than any justice had in the past 100 years.

and her audience at Duke know perfectly well that policy (law) is formally created by the government, but she was trying to point out how powerful judges can be with the decisions they make. Many experts agree that she was pretty much correct. Legal decisions can and do have influence on the way new laws are created. Some go as far as to say that the District, Circuit, and Supreme Courts create laws all the time. For Sonia to have actually said this out loud to an audience was risky, however. Her critics jumped all over the comment. They said it was proof that she's an activist judge who will try to legislate, or make laws, from the bench.

Vote of Confidence

At the end of the confirmation hearings—despite their confrontational and sometimes unfair questioning—things turned out just the way everyone had figured they would. The Republicans just didn't have enough votes to block Sonia from being confirmed to the Supreme Court and the Democrats had no intention of voting against her. On July 28, 2009, the Senate Judiciary Committee voted 13 to 6 to endorse Sonia's nomination. Twelve of those votes were from Democratic panel members; one came from the Republican camp.

Sonia Sotomayor had just become the 111th U.S. Supreme Court justice. Then she turned and gave her mom a hug.

Republican panel members, along with many other conservative groups, say Sonia is a softie who brings her own political agenda to the job. Sonia Sotomayor has many supporters in the Democratic Party. Democrats find her to be a qualified, moderate, and mainstream judge. They say her opinions and judgments are by the book, and deeply connected to the written law.

"Those who struggle to pin the label of judicial activist on Judge Sotomayor are met by

> "I, Sonia Sotomayor, do solemnly swear that I will administer justice without respect to persons, and do equal right to the poor and to the rich, and that I will faithfully and impartially discharge and perform all the duties incumbent upon me as Associate Justice of the Supreme Court of the United States under the Constitution and laws of the United States. So help me God."
>
> Sonia Sotomayor

her solid record of judging based on the law," said Senate Judiciary Committee Chairman Patrick Leahy from Vermont. "She is a restrained, experienced and thoughtful judge who has shown no biases in her rulings."

Many people believe Sonia's deliberations share a similar philosophical grounding with those of the retiring judge whose post she has filled, Justice David Souter. They feel she's not going to create any waves on the bench.

On August 6, 2009, the larger body of the Senate confirmed Sonia's nomination with a vote of 68 to 31. The vote was largely split down party lines, with all the Democrats voting in favor of Sonia's confirmation and all but nine Republicans voting against it.

With her confirmation, the White House noted that Sonia brought more federal justice experience to the Supreme Court than any justice had in the past 100 years.

Walking Through a Tidal Wave

It's a long road ahead for Justice Sonia Sotomayor. Retired Justice David Souter, the man whom Sonia replaced through his retirement, likened the experience to walking through a tidal wave. Justice

Judge Sonia Sotomayor is sworn in as the 111th Justice of the U.S. Supreme Court in the East Conference room of the Supreme Court building on August 8, 2009. Chief Justice John Roberts (right) administers the oath, as Sonia's mother, Celina, holds the Bible and her brother, Juan, looks on.

Stephen G. Breyer, who joined the court in 1994, said he was "frightened to death" for his first three years.

Even as far back as 1973, when Sonia was just fresh out high school, Justice William J. Brennan Jr., who served for longer than 30 years, had a warning for newcomers. He said that nothing in the whole world could prepare them for being a Supreme Court judge. He said it didn't matter how much prior experience they had as judges. The job was totally different than any other kind of judging job. Not for the faint of heart!

As with every other challenge she had faced before, Sonia was more than ready. With two oaths, and in two private ceremonies at the Supreme Court building, Sonia was sworn in by Chief Justice John G. Roberts Jr. just after 11:00 a.m. on August 8, 2009. Her many friends were present, as were her brother, Juan, and her mother, Celina.

Dressed in a striking suit and beaming with anticipation, Sonia Sotomayor placed her left hand on the bible and held her right hand high. In an even tone, she pledged the following to the population of the United States of America:

"I, Sonia Sotomayor, do solemnly swear that I will administer justice without respect to persons, and do equal right to the poor and to the rich, and that I will faithfully and impartially discharge and perform all the duties incumbent upon me as Associate Justice of the Supreme Court of the United States under the Constitution and laws of the United States. So help me God."

With that, she shook the Chief Justice's hand. Sonia Sotomayor had just become the 111th U.S. Supreme Court justice.

Then she turned and gave her mom a hug.

Justice Sonia Sotomayor gets a hug from her mother following a speech by President Barack Obama (right) honoring her appointment to the Supreme Court. The occasion was a reception for Sonia on August 12, 2009.

FIRST VOTE AS A JUSTICE

Sonia's first recorded vote cast on the Supreme Court was in a case involving the death penalty. She and three other Supreme Court judges voted to stay (prevent) the execution of an Ohio man.

To settle a dispute over a landscaping business, Jason Getsy had been hired in 1995 to kill Charles Serafino. Getsy shot Serafino seven times, but Serafino lived. Serafino's mother, Ann, however, was killed in the incident. Sonia and the other judges who voted to stay the execution agreed with Getsy's lawyer that it was unfair for him to be sentenced to death by lethal injection while the man who put the whole plan together (and hired Getsy to kill his rival) received a lesser sentence.

The final vote by the Supreme Court was 5 to 4. Getsy was put to death on August 18, 2009.

Chapter 8
The Person Behind the Robe

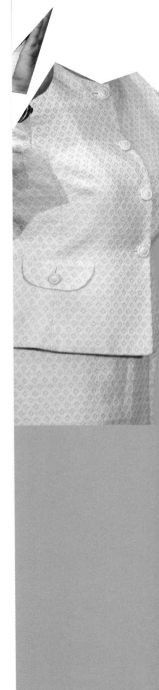

Sonia Sotomayor was perhaps one of the humblest judges ever invited to join the U.S. Supreme Court. Unlike many other judges, she didn't come from a wealthy family. There was no judicial legacy in her family. She had struggled against poverty and discrimination—and she had even found that she needed to teach herself how to write properly when she became an undergraduate at Princeton University.

Following a Different Path

"She had such a different path," said Robert H. Klonoff, dean of the Lewis & Clark Law School in Portland, Oregon. He knew this fact well, for Dean Klonoff had attended Yale with Sonia. Klonoff said she was different than so many of the other Supreme Court judges who rose to that position because of their pedigree:

"There were so many people that had Roman numerals after their names and long histories of family members who had gone to Yale, and here was this woman who was from the projects, not hiding her views at all, just totally outspoken. She's one of those where, even at a

school with great people, I knew that she was going to go on and do amazing things."

Someone Who Includes Everyone

Sonia has achieved considerable heights in the courtroom and in the field of law. There are, however, other facets of her professional life that show equal dedication and accomplishment. As an advocate for Latinos, she has always been willing to speak about her experience as a Latina and as a woman. Since 1993, she has given over 180 speeches at various events around the country. Many of these speeches focus on issues concerning gender or ethnicity. Many of her talks are delivered to women's or minority groups.

Always interested in breaking down barriers and getting to know "the little guy," she helped start a group at the courthouse to help people of the court come to know one another better. Realizing the power of positive role modeling and mentoring in shaping the next generation, Sonia also invited young women to the courthouse on Take Your Daughter to Work Day. Once a year, Sonia throws a Christmas party

Some Puerto Ricans say Sonia's success is as significant to their cultural legacy as President Obama's election was to African-Americans.

"Here came this woman who reinvigorated us with the idea that a Latina can have a lot to contribute, not just to their own group, but to the entire American society."

Arlene Davila, a New York University professor of anthropology and expert in Puerto Rican and Latino identity

The official portrait of Associate Justice Sonia Sotomayor

in the U.S. Court House. She invites everybody from clerks to counselors to custodians.

Sonia Sotomayor: Pride of Puerto Ricans!

They say it's the highest position a Puerto Rican has ever held in this country. For Sonia Sotomayor—one of their own—to have gained entry to the Supreme Court of the United States is truly a milestone.

Some Puerto Ricans say Sonia's success is as significant to their cultural legacy as President Obama's election was to African-Americans. Sonia's confirmation as a Supreme Court justice has boosted a sense of identity among Puerto Ricans in the continental United States, and came just in time. For years, the very borders of that Puerto Rican identity were being gradually worn away as the group was increasingly identified using the more general terms Hispanic and Latino.

Back in 1959, Edwin Torres became the first Puerto Rican assistant district attorney in New York. He might possibly have been the first Puerto Rican to achieve this level in the whole of the United States.

It was big news at the time, says Torres. The story of his accomplishment was splashed across the newspapers, and he was treated like a minor celebrity for a while. Torres went on to be elected to the New York State Supreme Court in 1980. Born in 1931, he still serves as a justice and is also a well-known and accomplished writer of crime fiction.

In the intervening years between Torres's achievement and Sonia's nomination to the

Supreme Court, Puerto Ricans made many great advances in the fields of business, the arts, and politics. Nobody, said Torres, would have thought that a Nuyorican woman from a poor, single-parent family would have made it to the top of the heap. "It is beyond anybody's

The wider U.S. society is starting to realize that Puerto Ricans have been gradually adding their voices and gifts to America's culture and economy.

imagination when I started that a Puerto Rican could ascend to that position, to the Supreme Court," said Torres.

Although many Puerto Ricans have indeed battled poverty and racism to climb to positions of influence across the country, many of those struggles have, until now, been invisible. Most people who rise above their background and achieve great things don't usually stick around in the projects. They leave, and they don't often come back. So that greatness gets dispersed—and as it disperses, it's hard to get a handle on just how many people have beat the odds and attained success.

Today, with all the public debate and

discussion surrounding Sonia's confirmation to the Supreme Court, many of the aspirational struggles of Puerto Ricans have finally come to light. The wider U.S. society is starting to realize that Puerto Ricans have been gradually adding their voices and gifts to America's culture and economy. Sonia Sotomayor brings a lot to the table—not just for Puerto Ricans, but for the U.S. population she serves.

Sonia has made her fellow Puerto Ricans proud. Her success is greeted with the loudest cheers, in the neighborhoods where she grew up. In the South Bronx and East Harlem, people get how much of a struggle it was for her to break away and achieve her dream. And the best part? She hasn't forgotten about where she came from. She didn't just up and walk away from her neighborhood when she reached her goals. She came back to tell people how she did it—and to guide their children in reaching their own dreams, too.

Finding That Work-Life Balance

Life as a judge is busy—busier than it is in most other professions. Add to that the fact that Sonia lives alone, so she isn't obligated to carve out time for a family. Passionate about her work, she often heads to the office seven days a week. She says sometimes she feels so busy it's hard for her to find time to sleep!

When she does relax, one of Sonia's favorite things to do is shop. She does her grocery shopping among the small specialty shops in Greenwich Village, where she lives in a two-bedroom condominium. She loves browsing the stores for ideas of what to give to other people, too. Perhaps because she can't often give the gift of her own time, giving other kinds of gifts brings her great pleasure. She helps support her mother, who now lives in Florida with her second husband.

Sonia also likes to travel. She returns to Puerto Rico once or twice a year, visiting relatives and sometimes giving speeches while she's there. "Although I am an American, love my country, and could achieve its opportunity of succeeding at anything I worked for, I also have a Latina soul and heart, with the magic that carries," she has said.

Some of Sonia's favorite Puerto Rican delicacies are pigs' feet with beans, a dish of mashed plantains called mofongo, and even pigs' tongue and ears! She loves the merengue music that accompanies her family get-togethers when she makes her return trips to the Caribbean homeland of her parents, and she says her family are all suckers for weepy Spanish love songs.

When Sonia was nominated to the Supreme Court, some critics claimed her diabetes made her an unsuitable candidate for the job. The White House

Judge Sonia Sotomayor poses with nephews Conner and Corey Sotomayor at Yankee Stadium in this undated family photograph.

was quick, however, to assure the country that Sonia's diabetes is well controlled. She takes care of her health, giving herself her own daily insulin injections. She works out three times a week on a treadmill and often leaves her white Saab parked in the garage in favor of walking to work. The Brooklyn Bridge is Sonia's favorite power-walking trail.

Though she never had children of her own, Sonia's brother has three children. She is a proud aunt and enjoys spending time with her extended family. She is the godmother of five other children, too. She mentors children from troubled neighborhoods and talks to her own mother every day. Although Sonia was raised Catholic, she doesn't attend mass on a regular basis—but she does go to church for special occasions.

Forever a New Yorker

Sonia enjoys the theater and attends the Metropolitan Opera. She likes the ballet, too. Down to earth as always, she's still a total fan of baseball. Her favorite team? Why, still the New York Yankees, of course! One of her former clerks, Melissa Murray, now a law professor at the University of California at Berkeley, recalled the time she went to a Yankees game with Sonia. Murray said Sonia bought tickets for seats in the bleachers,

Supreme Court Justice Sonia Sotomayor (right) gets what the New York Daily News *described as a "street salute" from sidewalk artist Hani Shihada in August 2009. The art drew compliments from New Yorkers on both the quality of the work and its subject!*

explaining that it was a more "authentic" experience that way. As she was doing this, Sonia was recognized by several people in the crowd. "We were on our way to the bleachers and people were like, 'Judge! Judge!'" said Murray. "She is really well known in the South Bronx and kind of a role model in the community."

Her brother Juan agrees that Sonia is a beloved fixture in her New York neighborhood. "If you had to describe my sister, you'd say New Yorker—it's her essence," said Juan. "I always joke that her vision does not extend beyond the Hudson River."

Never One to Rest on Her Laurels

Even with her local celebrity and all her notable professional accomplishments, Sonia remains humble to the end. Ever the achiever, she still believes she's got a long way to go— and a lot more to learn. "I have spent my years since Princeton, while at law school and in my various professional jobs, not feeling completely a part of the worlds I inhabit," she admitted. "I am always looking over my shoulder wondering if I measure up."

Twice a year, about 70 at-risk high school students get to experience the legal profession first-hand. Through the Development School for Youth Program, these kids attend 16 weeks of workshops designed to teach them numerous skills—but most importantly, how to function in the workplace.

At the end of the Development School for Youth Program, each student is given the opportunity to work a summer job at one of the corporate sponsors' organizations. Enjoyed by students and professionals alike, the experience "opens up possibilities that the students never dreamed of before," said Sonia.

Sonia Keeps on Leading: The Development School for Youth Program

Who's leading these workshops? Judge Sotomayor, of course, and a supporting cast of investment bankers and corporate executives. Sonia's own workshop in the Development School for Youth Program takes about 30 students through a complete trial of none other than a character known to children everywhere for her questionable judgment—Goldilocks. From her pool of students, Sonia hires six "lawyers" to help her. Through taking the roles of defense attorney, jurors, Goldilocks, and the prosecutor, students get to experience a full trial, from start to finish. Openings, closings, direct examinations, and cross examinations—it's all here!

Chronology

1954 Sonia Sotomayor is born in New York on June 25.

1962 At the age of eight, Sonia is diagnosed with type 1 diabetes.

1963 Sonia's father, Juan Sotomayor, dies of heart problems at the age of 42. His daughter, son, and wife are left to fend for themselves without him.

1963 At nine years of age, it dawns on Sonia that she wants to be a lawyer when she grows up, and maybe even a judge. She sticks to this goal throughout the rest of her school years.

1972 Sonia graduates at the top of her high school class. She delivers the valedictory address. She takes her friend and debating partner Ken Moy's advice and decides to pursue her bachelor's degree on a full scholarship at Princeton University in New Jersey.

1972–1976 Realizing that her English writing skills are not up to par, Sonia spends much of her first year at Princeton in the library and in private tutorials, learning how to write effectively. She majors in history at Princeton.

1974 In one of her first displays of student activism, Sonia, as part of the student group *Accion Puertorriqueno*, pens a letter to the New York Department office of the Federal Department of Health, Education and Welfare charging that Princeton is discriminating unfairly against minority students.

1976 On August 14, Sonia marries her high school sweetheart, Kevin Noonan. She graduates *summa cum laude* from Princeton and enrolls at Yale Law School, beginning her classes in the fall. She is again on a full scholarship.

1976—1979 Sonia attends Yale Law, earning a Juris Doctor degree.

1979 Sonia graduates from Yale. She takes a job as assistant district attorney for New York District Attorney Robert Morgenthau. She returns to New York, settling in Brooklyn.

1983 Sonia divorces Kevin Noonan.

1984 Sonia accepts a job at Pavia & Harcourt, a private law firm.

1991 On November 27, Sonia is nominated by the first President George Bush to a seat on the U.S. District Court.

1984—1992 Sonia works in private practice, investigating and trying cases involving counterfeit goods.

1992 Sonia is confirmed to the U.S. District Court for the Southern District of New York bench. In her 30s, Sonia is the youngest judge in the district, the first Hispanic federal judge in the state of New York, and the first Puerto Rican woman to serve as a federal judge.

1992–1998 Sonia works on the U.S. District Court, dealing with cases of fraud, white-collar crime, embezzlement, and drug smuggling. She relocates to the Bronx.

1995 Sonia gains renown for ending the baseball strike by ruling that owners were being unfair to players. Just one day before the new season begins, major league baseball resumes.

1997 In June, President Bill Clinton nominates Sonia to a seat on the U.S. Court of Appeals for the Second Circuit.

1998 After a bit of a political disagreement, Sonia is confirmed on October 2.

1998–2009 Sonia hears over 3,000 cases as a judge on the Court of Appeals for the Second Circuit. In this time, she writes over 380 well-thought-out opinions.

1998 Sonia becomes engaged to New York construction contractor Peter White, but the engagement is broken in 2000.

2001 In an address to the graduating class at U of California at Berkeley, Sonia makes her now infamous comment about how a "wise Latina" would probably reach different conclusions on the bench than a privileged white male.

2005 Sonia is suggested to President George W. Bush as a candidate for Supreme Court. He dismisses the idea, not wanting to nominate a "liberal" judge during his term as president.

2009 Sonia and one other judge on the Second Circuit court panel rule against white firefighters, who claim their employer was practicing discrimination in fitness testing. Numerous other judges question the ruling. The decision is overturned by the Supreme Court. On May 26, President Barack Obama nominates Sonia to the Supreme Court. On July 13, Sonia's confirmation hearings before the Senate Judiciary Committee begin. On July 28, the Senate Judiciary Committee votes 13 to 6 to endorse Sonia's nomination. Sonia brings to the Supreme Court more experience as a federal justice than any other nominee in more than 100 years. On August 8, Sonia is sworn in as a Supreme Court justice. On August 18, Sonia casts her first vote as a Supreme Court justice. Along with three other justices, she votes to stay an execution. They lose. A vote of five to four means the man will receive the death penalty.

Glossary

activist Someone who tries to bring about social, political, economic, or environmental change by trying to persuade others to change their behavior

adjudicated Ruled on; decided

advocacy Pleading or working toward the support of a cause

advocacy initiatives Proposals for new laws which support specific causes

affirmative action Employment, education, and other policies that take into account an applicant's race, income, health, or physical disabilities in an attempt to promote equal opportunity

agenda A set of issues that a person or group wishes to address or influence through their actions

alumni People who at one time attended a given school, college or university

analytical Able to see every aspect of an argument or issue from many sides in a calm and nonbiased manner

arbitration A hearing to resolve a dispute between two parties, overseen by someone recognized to have authority to make a decision

aspiration A goal or strong desire

common law Laws that are made by court decisions as opposed to statutes

confirmation The act of confirming, or making certain, a given person's status

conservative A political thought structure that holds that traditional institutions (such as church and family) are the ideal, and that radical change should be avoided in society. The emphasis is on stability as opposed to change.

counterfeiter Someone who illegally creates copies of authentic objects, such as Gucci watches, and sells them cheaply

deliberations The weighing and examination of facts in a case in order to come to some conclusion

discharged Relieved of performing military services

discrimination Unfair treatment of a person or a group based on characteristics such as age, race, ethnic background, social class, or physical condition

district attorney An elected or appointed official who represents the government in the prosecution of criminal offenses

embezzlement A type of fraud that involves secretly stashing away money that belongs to someone else (say, an employer or a client) so that the other person is unaware of it

empathy The ability to understand another person's situation or share his or her feelings

felonies Serious crimes, such as rape, murder, or robbery, that are punishable by imprisonment or even death

fraud Intentional deception (such as lying) by a person or one party for personal gain or in order to damage the reputation of a person or another party. Fraud is considered a crime.

hardscrabble Characterized by hardship, poverty, and gaining little reward for a lot of hard work

impartiality Freedom from bias or favoritism

intellectual property Ownership of a person's creative ideas, such as music or art

irrevocable A decision that cannot be canceled or reversed

Ivy League A group of eight private post-secondary institutions in the United States, including Harvard, Yale, Brown, Columbia, Cornell, Princeton, Dartmouth College, and the University of Pennsylvania

liberal Supportive of social change with a view toward creating a more equal society

litigants Parties engaged in a lawsuit

mentor A trusted friend, counselor, or teacher who advises and provides an example for a less experienced person

nomination Part of the process of selecting or announcing someone for a certain role or office

philosophical Relating to a person's beliefs, convictions, and principles

quota Numerical requirements for hiring, admitting, graduating, or promoting members of a particular racial or ethnic group. Quotas are usually established as a means to reduce discrimination, but sometimes have the opposite effect of intensifying discrimination.

radical Extreme or beyond traditional in thought or practice

scholarship A financial award to be used in paying for a student's tuition at an academic institution

Senate confirmation hearings The process of the Senate confirming or denying the president's nomination of someone to a high-ranking position

stringent Strict, precise, or exacting

successor Someone who comes after

summa cum laude A Latin term meaning "with highest honor"

transcripts A written record of trial proceedings, word for word

unanimous With all parties agreeing on the same thing

valedictorian Highest-ranked student among the graduating class. The valedictorian usually is the final speaker at the graduation ceremony.

Further Information

Books

Felix, Antonia. *Sonia Sotomayor: The True American Dream.*
New York, NY: Penguin Group, 2010.

McElroy, Lisa Tucker. *Sonia Sotomayor: First Hispanic U.S. Supreme Court Justice.* Minneapolis, MN: Lerner Publications, 2010.

Reed, Patrick K. *Judge Sonia Sotomayor: Selected Opinions (Laws and Legislation).* Hauppauge, NY: Nova Science Publishers, Inc., 2010.

Thomas, Tom. *And Then There Were Three: Sonia Sotomayor's Climb to be the Third Woman Justice of the Supreme Court.*
Los Angeles, CA: CreateSpace, 2009.

Winter, Jonah. *Sonia Sotomayor: A Judge Grows in the Bronx.*
New York, NY: Atheneum Books, 2009.

Female Force: Sonia Sotomayor. BlueWater Comics, 2010.
Vancouver, WA:

Web sites

http://topics.nytimes.com/top/reference/timestopics/people/s/sonia_sotomayor/index.html?inline=nyt-per
This Web site gives an overview of Sonia Sotomayor's life, including her nomination to the Supreme Court, the process of her confirmation, her childhood and growing-up years, and some of her most notable legal decisions.

www.cbc.ca/world/story/2009/05/26/f-sotomayor.html
From CBC comes background about Supreme Court justice Sonia Sotomayor, including links to her opening statement at her confirmation hearing.

www.nytimes.com/interactive/2000/05/26/us/politics/20090526_SOTOMAYOR_TIMELINE.html
An interactive timeline shows readers Sonia Sotomayor's life and career with captioned photos. Additional articles appear as links. Sonia's notable cases, recent news stories, and video clips are included in the interactive timeline.

www.supremecourthistory.org/index.htm
This site is hosted by the Supreme Court Historical Society. Readers can learn about the operations of the current court and read biographies of all the justices sitting on the nation's highest court. Includes photos, publications, and rich historical documentation.

http://sotomayorforjustice.com/
The Mexican-American Legal Defense and Educational Fund endorsed Sonia Sotomayor as a candidate for the Supreme Court. On this site, readers will find news and video updates, a biography, and a selection of speeches and comments made by Sonia Sotomayor on such issues as civil rights, women's issues, and immigration.

www.supremecourt.gov/
This site is maintained by the Supreme Court of the United States. It features recent filings, opinions, bar admissions, judge bios, court rules, visiting information, and other interesting court-related information.

www.allstars.org/content/joseph-forgione-development-school-youth
The Joseph A. Forgione Development School for Youth website gives readers a glimpse into this mentoring program for inner-city youth. (Sonia Sotomayor leads students in a mock trial workshop where youth follow Goldilocks through criminal proceedings.) Application packages are available to download.

www.topuertorico.org/index.shtml
Maintained by Magaly Rivera, Welcome to Puerto Rico offers information about Puerto Rico's government, history, economy, climate, culture and recipes. Many links are available for those who wish to do further research into this tropical U.S. territory.

http://pewhispanic.org/
The Pew Hispanic Center features research into demographic and economic trends, issues surrounding education, immigration and identity, and a wealth of publications and links concerning the U.S. Hispanic population.

Index

acceptance of all people 28, 40, 77, 78, 94
Accion Puertorriqueno 34-35
activism
　accusations about 78, 86, 87
　political 34-35, 65, 66
Adams, James Truslow 13
advocating for others 41, 46, 65, 94
American Bar Association 61
American Dream, the 11-12, 13, 73, 75
appeals 9, 61
　Court of, for the Second Circuit 61-62, 63, 64-70, 71
　Ricci v. DeStefano case 67-69
Associate Justices 10, 11
awards 36

baseball 22, 40
　Sonia's love for 22, 40, 100
　strike 56, 58
being prepared 44, 55, 57, 71, 80
boards
　Sonia served on 46
　what they do 49
branches of U.S. government 9
breaking down barriers 94

Bush
　President George H.W. 51
　President George W. 73

Chicanos/Chicanas 15
Chief Justice 10, 11
childhood 19-20, 21, 23, 24, 25, 26-28
class valedictorian 26, 28
Clinton, President Bill 61, 62
confirmation hearings 12, 78-80, 81, 82, 86-87, 88
connection to her community 17, 74, 76, 97-98
counterfeiters 46, 47
crime rate in New York 43, 45
critics 57, 61-62, 65, 76, 78, 81

D'Amato, Senator Alfonse M. 62
debating skills 28, 39
Development School for Youth Program 103
diabetes 22, 24, 99-100
discrimination, 22, 33, 65
　against minorities 33, 34-35, 39, 65
　against women 31-32, 65

education 26-27
　college 22
　importance of 20, 25
　improving writing skills 32, 34
　Princeton University 31-32, 33, 34-36
　reading 24, 34
　Yale University 38, 39, 40
empathy 14, 76, 78, 79, 106
equality 12
Executive branch 9

family
　brother Juan 24, 29, 88, 89, 90, 99, 100
　father Juan 19, 21, 23
　in housing projects 25, 26-27
　husband Kevin Noonan 37, 44
　mother Celina 19, 20, 21, 23, 25, 27, 29, 89 91, 99
　relatives 98, 99

hardships 20, 24
Hispanics 14-16
housing projects 25, 26-27

influences 20, 29
interests 98-100

judge career
  applying the law as it is written 55, 65, 78, 79, 82, 87
  becoming a judge 51
  consequences of her decisions 66
  controversial ruling 68-69
  ending 1995 baseball strike 56, 59
  hearing cases 55-56
  her reputation 55, 57, 67
  law clerks 74, 76
  liberal-conservative leanings 62, 78
  personal experiences shaping 64-65
  promotion to U.S. District Court 51-52
  Ricci v. DeStefano case 68-69
  rulings 67-70
  United States Court of Appeals for the Second Circuit 61-62, 64-70, 71
  writing opinions 71
judges
  being impartial 64
  female in the U.S. 54
  power of 26, 86
Judicial branch 9
justice statue 4

Latinos/Latinas 14, 15-16, 65, 94, 95
  students 31, 40
  "wise Latina" statement 65, 80

lawyer career
  being in front of judges 43-44, 45
  with D.A. Robert Morgenthau 43, 45
  making partner 48
  number of years in 51
  at Pavia & Harcourt 44, 46, 47, 48, 52
  prosecuting attorney 43-44, 45, 46
  working toward a 26, 40
lawyers
  Edwin Torres 96
  female 54-55
  recruiting 39
  Shaw, Pittman, Potts & Trowbridge 39
  what they do 41
Legislative branch 9
loneliness 37, 54

Mexican-Americans 15, 23, 35
minorities 22, 32, 65
  discrimination against 33, 34-35, 36, 39
Morgenthau, D.A. Robert 43, 45
Moynihan, Senator Daniel Patrick 51

nominations
  confirmation hearings 11, 12, 78-80, 81, 82, 86-87
  reasons for 11, 81
  to Supreme Court 5-6, 8, 11, 29, 73, 74-75, 76, 78-80, 81, 82, 86-87
  to U.S. Court of Appeals 61, 62, 63, 64
Nuyoricans 19, 96

Obama, President Barack 5, 7, 10, 14, 17, 73, 74-75, 78, 80
original jurisdiction 9

Pavia, George 73
Pavia & Harcourt 44, 46, 47, 48, 52
Perry Mason show 26
personal life 37, 98-100, 102
poverty 23, 25, 32, 51, 96-97
Princeton University 31-32, 33, 34-36
Puerto Ricans 14, 15-16, 19, 22, 23, 36
  Edwin Torres 96, 97
  Nuyoricans 19, 97
  successes of 96-98

qualities 12, 28, 44, 65, 80, 81, 82, 87, 100

racism 13, 15-16, 20, 22, 38, 65, 81
reading 22, 24, 34
Republican senators 61, 62, 76, 78, 79, 80, 81, 82
Ricci v. DeStefano case 68-69
Roberts Jr, Chief Justice John G. 10
role model 94, 100

Index

salary 52
scholarships 31, 38
Senate Judiciary
 Committee 51, 64,
 73, 79, 83, 87
Shaw, Pittman, Potts &
 Trowbridge 39
Souter, Justice David
 6, 29, 88
speeches 94
State of New York
 Mortgage Agency 46
strikes
 baseball 56, 59
 labor 15
supporters 65, 87
Supreme Court
 building 9, 11
 history of 11

Jason Getsy's case 90
joining the 84, 88
junior justice job 84
justices 9, 54
nomination to 5-6, 8,
 11, 12, 29, 73, 74-75,
 76, 78-80, 81, 82,
 86-87
number of members
 9, 11
portrait 85
purpose of 9
ruling on Ricci v.
 DeStefano case
 68-69
salaries of justices 10
voting Sonia into
 86, 87

women justices in
 54, 55
swearing-in ceremonies
 10, 14, 89, 90, 91

teaching jobs 54, 71, 102

United States Court of
 Appeals for the Second
 Circuit 61-62, 63,
 64-70, 71

voting power 16

wisdom 65
"wise Latina" statement
 65, 80

Yale University 38, 39, 40

About the Author

Alex Van Tol is the author of two teen novels and two biographies. She taught middle school for eight years but turned to writing full-time after having her second child. Alex writes for magazines, web sites, and corporations. She lives with her husband and two sons, where they seize every possible opportunity to hang out at the beach.